THE LITTLE

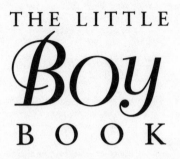
Boy

BOOK

Paula Yates

Virgin

First published in Great Britain in 1994 by
Virgin Books
an imprint of Virgin Publishing Ltd
332 Ladbroke Grove
London W10 5AH

A catalogue record for this book is available from the
British Library

ISBN 1 85227 481 6

Designed by Tony Paine
Illustrations by Diana Fisher

Typeset by Phoenix Photosetting, Chatham, Kent
Printed and bound in Great Britain by
Bath Press Ltd

Begin, little boy, to recognise your mother
with a smile.

Virgil

First Sightings

Name ....

....

Place of birth ....

Time and date of birth ....

....

Colour of hair ....

Colour of eyes ....

Weight at birth ....

Height at birth ....

First tooth ....

How Baby first moved along ....

....

When Baby first moved along ....

....

First words ....

....

First steps..

MEMORIES

Favourite song ....

Favourite toy ....

Favourite story ....

....

Favourite games ....

....

First party ....

....

Favourite foods ....

....

Favourite animal ....

Favourite clothes ....

....

First friend ....

First holiday ....

Funny sayings ....

....

SCHOOL DAYS

First day at school ....

Best friends ....

....

Favourite teacher ....

First play ....

Part played and words spoken ....

....

First sports day ....

Races run ....

Favourite activity ....

....

Least liked activity ....

....

First party without accompanying adult ....

....

Funny sayings ....

....

INTRODUCTION
by Paula Yates

I have never actually had a little boy, but my friend in the countryside has had two. The last time she was giving birth she was given large amounts of gas and air and when her son finally popped out she shouted rather dramatically to her husband, 'Oh, it's a lamb chop, and I wanted a chicken,' which I have always felt must rather sum it up.

Since then her two boys have been great friends with my three daughters, and during the many long summer days they have spent together at our house, I've had a great deal of time to study the differences between the sexes in those early years. Lock a girl into a vegetable garden and she doesn't re-emerge through the kitchen window daubed with mud

and shooting you with a courgette, for example. Nor do small boys employ the sort of brain-numbing power games that little girls seem adept at almost as soon as they can stagger around and fall headfirst into the paddling pool. Little boys, I have found, love building dens for hours, knocking nails in all over the place and whistling, while little girls (rather frighteningly, for any of us who believe in conditioning) scuttle around providing cups and saucers and putting biscuits on to large leaves.

I first had the idea of compiling this book when I was in the hospital having my last daughter, Pixie, and a friend arrived with an old Truby King child-care manual from the thirties. Oh, how I cried, deliciously torturing myself reading bits here and there and then clutching the tiny baby to my bosom vowing fervently that her life would be different; no one was giving *me* a heartbreaking little graph telling me I should only pick baby up for one hour out of each day.

But it was also apparent that anyone who plans a baby, is expecting a baby, likes babies

12

or has just had one has a tendency to become a bit of a baby bore. Of course the people who call you that are invariably men with large red faces like smacked bottoms who harbour ambitions to sneak off in their lunch hours to have vasectomies, but there is an element of truth in it. And I found I wanted to read more about babies – little boys who had endured Victorian rigours, little boys who had grown into great statesmen, and little boys who had simply inspired their mothers and fathers to write poems and prose just singing their praises. . . .

So here it is – the book I wanted to read. I hope you'll enjoy it as much as I did.

First
Sightings

He [Bogart] didn't know what kind of father he'd make. He was so afraid our closeness and incredible happiness together would be cut into by a child – but of course he wanted us to have a baby more than anything in the world, so he just would have to get used to the idea. He'd spent forty-eight years childless, and had never really considered that being a father would ever become a reality at this point in his life . . .

Two days before I was to bring my baby home, Los Angeles had its first snowfall in fifty years. I remember sitting in my hospital bed and looking out the window – I thought I was imagining things. What a great dividend – only right for the child of Eastern-born parents! I couldn't wait to get home. I could have a baby every nine months if it was this easy! I hoped Bogie was as happy as I was. As for me, I knew that I had it all – Bogie had given it to me.

On 11 January the ambulance took Steve and me home. As we were carried to the front door, there on the lawn was an enormous snowman which Bogie had spent half the night building. It was odd to see snow covering

camellia bushes. I was taken to our bedroom,
Steve to his at the other end of the house. We
had an intercom rigged so that I could hear
every sound in the nursery – could talk to the
nurse if I wished. It was kept on at all times. . .

My first morning home, I was having
breakfast in bed when Bogie went off to work.
Before he left, he stopped in to see his son – I
had the intercom on and suddenly heard in a
soft, new voice, 'Hello, son. You're a little
fella, aren't you? I'm Father. Welcome home.'

Lauren Bacall, By Myself by Lauren Bacall

Children are what their mothers are:
No fonder father's fondest care
Can fashion the infant's heart
As those creative beams that dart
With all their hopes and fear, upon
The cradle of a sleeping son.

Walter Savage Landor

My father almost died the day he was born. He came into the world fighting for his life. He was thirteen and a half pounds at birth, a big baby lodged inside a tiny woman less than five feet tall. The doctor had trouble getting him out. The doctor tugged away with forceps, ripping the baby's ear, cheek and neck and producing scars he would always carry. The newborn did not breathe. Thinking him dead, the doctor turned instead to treat the mother. The baby's grandmother scooped him up and held him under cold running water. *Life.*

Frank Sinatra, My Father by Nancy Sinatra

A man who has been the indisputable favourite of his mother keeps for life the feeling of a conqueror, that confidence of success that often induces real success.

Sigmund Freud

Here is Edward Bear, coming downstairs now, bump, bump, bump, on the back of his head, behind Christopher Robin. It is, as far as he knows, the only way of coming downstairs, but sometimes he feels that there really is another way, if only he could stop bumping for a moment and think of it. And then he feels that perhaps there isn't. Anyhow, here he is at the bottom, and ready to be introduced to you. Winnie-the-Pooh.

When I first heard his name, I said, just as you are going to say, 'But I thought he was a boy?'

'So did I,' said Christopher Robin.

'Then you can't call him Winnie?'

'I don't.'

'But you said –'

'He's Winnie-ther-Pooh. Don't you know what *"ther"* means?'

'Ah, yes, now I do,' I said quickly; and I hope you do too, because it is all the explanation you are going to get.

Winnie-the-Pooh by A. A. Milne

Twinkle, twinkle, little star,
How I wonder what you are!
Up above the world so high,
Like a diamond in the sky!

When the blazing sun is gone,
When he nothing shines upon,
Then you show your little light,
Twinkle, twinkle all the night.

Then the traveller in the dark
Thanks you for your little spark.
He could not tell which way to go,
If you did not twinkle so.

In the dark blue sky you keep,
And often through my curtains peep;
For you never shut your eye,
Till the sun is in the sky.

If the mother was

Rosy and merry	Pale and pensive
Heavier on the right side and carrying high	Heavier on the left side and carrying low
Of cool and humid temperament	Of dry and hot temperament

If the mother had

Pains on the right side of the womb	Pains on the left side of the womb
The right breast harder and firmer	The left breast larger
Red, hard, raised nipples	Paler, more drooping nipples
Thick white milk oozing from the breast	Pale, dilute milk

then

It would be a boy	It would be a girl

History of Childbirth by Jacques Gelis

I KNOW A BABY

I know a baby, such a baby,
Round blue eyes and cheeks of pink,
Such an elbow furrowed with dimples,
Such a wrist where creases sink.

'Cuddle and love me, cuddle and love me,'
Crows the mouth of coral pink:
Oh the bald head, and oh the sweet lips,
And oh the sleepy eyes that wink!

Christina Rossetti

When the nurse took my first child and put him to my breast his tiny mouth opened and reached for me as if he had known forever what to do. He began to suck with such force it took my breath away. It was like being attached to a vacuum cleaner . . .

Tears of joy ran shamelessly down my cheeks while he sucked. I thought back to my past conviction that only when I had a baby

would I *know* whatever it was I had to know.
Now I *did* know. It is the only important
thing I have ever learned, and so ridiculously
simple: love exists. It's real and honest and
unbelievably solid in a world where far too
much is complex or confusing or false.

Leslie Kenton

Mira, as thy dear Edward's senses grow,
Be sure they all will seek this point – *to know*;
Woo to enquiry – strictures long avoid;
By force the thirst of weakly sense is cloyed;
Silent attend the frown, the gaze, the smile,
To grasp far objects the incessant toil;
So play life's springs with energy, and try
The unceasing thirst of knowledge to supply.

I saw the beauteous Caleb t' other day
Stretch forth his little hand to touch a spray,
Whilst on the grass his drowsy nurse inhaled
The sweets of Nature as her sweets exhaled:
But, ere the infant reached the playful leaf,

She pulled him back – His eyes o'erflowed with
    grief;
He checked his tears – Her fiercer passions
    strove,
She looked a vulture cowering o'er a dove!
'I'll teach you, brat!' The pretty trembler
    sighed –
When, with a cruel shake, she hoarsely cried –
'Your mother spoils you – every thing you see
You covet. It shall ne'er be so with me!
Here, eat this cake, sit still, and don't you rise –
Why don't you pluck the sun down from the
    skies?
I'll spoil your sport – Come, laugh me in the
    face –
And henceforth learn to keep your proper place.
You rule me in the house! – To hush your noise
I, like a spaniel, must run for toys:
But here, Sir, let the trees alone, nor cry –
Pluck if you dare – Who's master? you, or I?'
    O brutal force, to check th' enquiring mind,
When it would pleasure in a rosebud find!

from *To Mira, On the Care of Her Infant*
by Ann Yearsley

Golden slumbers kiss your eyes,
Smiles awake you when you rise.
Sleep, pretty wantons; do not cry,
And I will sing a lullaby:
Rock them, rock them, lullaby.

Care is heavy, therefore sleep you;
You are care, and care must keep you.
Sleep, pretty wantons; do not cry,
And I will sing a lullaby:
Rock them, rock them, lullaby.

Thomas Dekker

TO WILLIAM SHELLEY

Thy little footsteps on the sands
Of a remote and lonely shore;
The twinkling of thine infant hands,
Where now the worm will feed no more;
Thy mingled look of love and glee
When we returned to gaze on thee.

Percy Bysshe Shelley

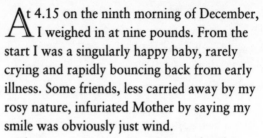

At 4.15 on the ninth morning of December, I weighed in at nine pounds. From the start I was a singularly happy baby, rarely crying and rapidly bouncing back from early illness. Some friends, less carried away by my rosy nature, infuriated Mother by saying my smile was obviously just wind.

I have no reason to question my family's assessment of me as the most adorable of infants, but such perfection just doesn't exist.

During my father's infancy, the worry had been about his solemn mien and dark skin shade. My appeal was tempered by the fact that I had no hair! Although Mother would hold my head up to the light to persuade doubters that the fuzz would eventually become real hair, I remained billiard-ball bald for nearly two years.

Douglas Fairbanks Jr

Tentzin Gyatso's mother, who died in 1981, remembered a difficult pregnancy. Her husband, who died when the god-king was twelve, had to take to his bed at that time, and no one could discover the source of his illness. But as soon as the baby was born he was up and about again, none the weaker and ready to resume his many tasks around the modest farmstead without delay. On the night before the birth, she had had an old dream; two blue dragons came to greet her in the most formal manner.

The Dalai Lama: A Biography
by Claude B. Levenson

Monday's child is fair of face,
Tuesday's child is full of grace,
Wednesday's child is full of woe,
Thursday's child has far to go,
Friday's child is loving and giving,
Saturday's child works hard for a living,
But the child that is born on the Sabbath day
Is bonny and blithe, and good and gay.

B ut your new baby has come to stay. It is well for you to know in advance that he will sometimes be troublesome and annoying . . .

All this means is that even the best of good fathers, in spite of loving their children, are quite humanly often inconvenienced and annoyed by them.

Fathers are Parents Too
by O. Spurgeon English MD

Upon my lap my sovereign sits
And sucks upon my breast.
Meanwhile his love sustains my life,
And gives my body rest.
Sing lullaby, my little boy,
Sing lullaby, my only joy.

When thou hast taken thy repast,
Repose, my babe, on me;
So may thy mother and thy nurse
Thy cradle also be.
Sing lullaby, my little boy,
Sing lullaby, my only joy.

28

I grieve that duty doth not work
All what my wishing would,
Because I would not be to thee
But in the best I should.
Sing lullaby, my little boy,
Sing lullaby, my only joy.

Yet as I am, and as I may,
I must and will be thine,
Though all too little for thyself,
Vouchsafing to be mine.
Sing lullaby, my little boy,
Sing lullaby, my only joy.

Richard Verstegan

Sweet Benedict, whilst thou art young,
And know'st not yet the use of tongue,
Keep it in thrall whilst thou art free:
Imprison it or it will thee.

John Hoskyns

29

During the winter of '38 when Ethel was carrying me, she had the habit of wetting her finger and fixing Dad's long sideburns into shape. The nurses at Bancroft Road Maternity Hospital did much the same to me, so instead of seeing a 'fluffed-up' head like all the other newcomers, my relatives came upon a 'little old man', complete with parting and Victorian hairstyle, peering out from my mother's side. My Auntie Julie, who was to become my godmother, thought it 'romantic', but as the first grandchild of both families, Ethel being the eldest Perrott and Tom the Stamps' firstborn, both Cockney clans were only too pleased to endow me with anything special.

Stamp Album by Terence Stamp

Hush-a-bye, Baby, on the tree top,
When the wind blows the cradle will rock;
When the bough breaks the cradle will fall,
Down will come baby, and cradle, and all.

MARION'S BABY

There he lay upon his back,
The yearling creature, warm and moist with life
To the bottom of his dimples – and to the ends
Of the lovely tumbled curls about his face;
For since he had been covered over much
To keep him from the light-glare, both his
    cheeks
Were hot and scarlet as the first live rose
The shepherd's heart-blood ebbed away into
The faster for his love. And love was here
As instant; in the pretty baby-mouth,
Shut close as if for dreaming that it sucked,
The little naked feet, drawn up the way
Of nestled birdlings; everything so soft
And tender – to the tiny holdfast hands
Which, closing on a finger into sleep,
Had kept a mould of't.

From *Aurora Leigh*
by Elizabeth Barrett Browning

He made his bound before he saw what it was he was jumping at, and then he tried to stop himself. The result was that he shot up straight into the air for four or five feet, landing almost where he left ground.

'Man!' he snapped. 'A man's cub. Look!'

Directly in front of him, holding on by a low branch, stood a naked brown baby who could just walk – as soft and as dimpled a little atom as ever came to a wolf's cave at night. He looked up into Father Wolf's face, and laughed.

'Is that a man's cub?' said Mother Wolf. 'I have never seen one. Bring it here.'

A wolf accustomed to moving his own cubs can, if necessary, mouth an egg without breaking it, and though Father Wolf's jaws closed right on the child's back not a tooth even scratched the skin, as he laid it down among the cubs.

'How little! How naked, and – how bold!' said Mother Wolf softly. The baby was pushing his way between the cubs to get close to the warm hide. '*Ahai!* He is taking his meal with the others. And so this is a man's cub. Now,

was there ever a wolf that could boast of a
man's cub among her children?'

The Jungle Books by Rudyard Kipling

A CRADLE SONG

The angels are stooping
Above your bed;
They weary of trooping
With the whimpering dead.

God's laughing in Heaven
To see you so good;
The Sailing Seven
Are gay with His mood.

I sigh that kiss you,
For I must own
That I shall miss you
When you have grown.

W. B. Yeats

Lullaby, Lullaby,
Shadows creep across the sky.
See, the sun has gone to rest,
Lullaby.

Lullaby, Lullaby,
Little one to Dreamland fly,
Till the morning sun awakes,
Lullaby.

Phyllis Garlick

What are little boys made of?
What are little boys made of?
Frogs and snails,
And puppy-dogs' tails,
That's what little boys are made of.

What are little girls made of?
What are little girls made of?
Sugar and spice,
And all things nice,
That's what little girls are made of.

34

REMEMBRANCES
OF CHILDHOOD

PAST AND PRESENT

I remember, I remember
The house where I was born,
The little window where the sun
Came peeping in at morn;
He never came a wink too soon
Nor brought too long a day;
But now, I often wish the night
Had borne my breath away.

I remember, I remember
The roses, red and white,
The violets, and the lily-cups –
Those flowers made of light!
The lilacs where the robin built,
And where my brother set
The laburnum on his birthday, –
The tree is living yet!

I remember, I remember
Where I was used to swing,
And thought the air must rush as fresh
To swallows on the wing;
My spirit flew in feathers then

That is so heavy now,
And summer pools could hardly cool
The fever on my brow.

I remember, I remember
The fir trees dark and high;
I used to think their slender tops
Were close against the sky:
It was a childish ignorance,
But now 'tis little joy
To know I'm farther off from Heaven
Than when I was a boy.

Thomas Hood

WHOLE DUTY OF CHILDREN

A child should always say what's true,
And speak when he is spoken to,
And behave mannerly at table:
At least as far as he is able.

Robert Louis Stevenson

Strawberry Fields is a real place. After I stopped living at Penny Lane, I moved in with my auntie who lived in the suburbs in a nice semi-detached place with a small garden and doctors and lawyers and that ilk living around – not the poor slummy kind of image that was projected in all the Beatles stories. In the class system, it was about half a class higher than Paul, George and Ringo, who lived in government-subsidised housing. We owned our house and had a garden. They didn't have anything like that. Near that home was Strawberry Fields, a house near a boys' reformatory where I used to go to garden parties as a kid with my friends Nigel and Pete. We would go there and hang out and sell lemonade bottles for a penny. We always had fun at Strawberry Fields.

John Lennon

LINES AND SQUARES

Whenever I walk in a London street,
I'm ever so careful to watch my feet;
   And I keep in the squares,
   And the masses of bears,
Who wait at the corners all ready to eat
The sillies who tread on the lines of the street,
   Go back to their lairs,
   And I say to them, 'Bears,
Just look how I'm walking in all of the squares!'

And the little bears growl to each other, 'He's
   mine,
As soon as he's silly and steps on a line.'
And some of the bigger bears try to pretend
That they came round the corner to look for a
   friend;
And they try to pretend that nobody cares
Whether you walk on the lines or squares.
But only the sillies believe their talk;
It's ever so portant how you walk.
And it's ever so jolly to call out, 'Bears,
Just watch me walking in all the squares!'

A. A. Milne

A CHILD'S THOUGHT

At seven, when I go to bed,
I find such pictures in my head:
Castles with dragons prowling round,
Gardens where magic fruits are found;
Fair ladies prisoned in a tower,
Or lost in an enchanted bower;
While gallant horsemen ride by streams
That border all this land of dreams
I find, so clearly in my head
At seven, when I go to bed.

At seven, when I wake again,
The magic land I seek in vain;
A chair stands where the castle frowned,
The carpet hides the garden ground,
No fairies trip across the floor,
Boots, and not horsemen, flank the door,
And where the blue streams rippling ran
Is now a bath and water-can;
I seek the magic land in vain
At seven, when I wake again.

                                        Robert Louis Stevenson

One day, . . . we found a dead mouse lying among our treasures. It was an exciting discovery. Thwaites took it out by its tail and waved it in front of our faces. 'What shall we do with it?' he cried.

'It stinks!' someone shouted. 'Throw it out of the window quick!'

'Hold on a tick,' I said. 'Don't throw it away.'

Thwaites hesitated. They all looked at me.

When writing about oneself, one must strive to be truthful. Truth is more important than modesty. I must tell you, therefore, that it was I and I alone who had the idea for the great and daring Mouse Plot. We all have our moments of brilliance and glory, and this was mine.

'Why don't we', I said, 'slip it into one of Mrs Pratchett's jars of sweets? Then when she puts her dirty hand in to grab a handful, she'll grab a stinky dead mouse instead.'

The other four stared at me in wonder. Then, as the sheer genius of the plot began to sink in, they all started grinning. They slapped me on the back. They cheered me and danced around the classroom. 'We'll do it today!' they cried. 'We'll do it on the way home! *You* had the idea,' they said to me, 'so *you* can be the one to put the mouse in the jar.'

Boy: *Tales of Childhood* by Roald Dahl

The next afternoon I found another opportunity to slip downstairs again. When my mother asked where I was going I told her I wanted to listen to the goblins who burbled to each other in the water tank in the basement – a frightening fiction of the caretaker's wife. For some reason I wished to keep my friendship with the lady in the Ground Floor Front a secret.

This time when I knocked the door was opened from the inside immediately; she stood there in a flowered dressing-gown, fluffy slippers and a large embroidered shawl round her shoulders. She clapped her hands in welcome. 'Sit down, I am going to dance for you.'

I curled up on the old squashy sofa with a lot of dusty cushions.

'You will have to imagine the music. We are in a big theatre. Drury Lane.'

She picked up a waste-paper basket, put it on her head, raised her arms high and started to hum. Her arms began to undulate slowly.

'Do you hear the fiddles?'

'No.'

'Use your imagination, boy! Hark at the cymbals! And the tinkling bells. And here come the drums! You must applaud, boy. Clap your hands!'

Blessings in Disguise by Alec Guinness

When I was very, very young I used to listen to everything from the BBC to Radio Luxembourg. If a child is musical, you can see that in children of two years old, especially nowadays. You'll see some children of two years old dance and others that don't, which doesn't mean to say that they'll become musicians – just that they're aware of music and, by the time they're around three, they'll distinguish between the kind of music they like and the kind they don't.

You see, we didn't have a record player at home and my immediate family wasn't really musical, and Chris was only about two at the time and as far as I was concerned he was nothing more than a punch bag and I used to beat him up regularly, but then that's quite a common thing with brothers.

It wasn't until I was about twelve that I became really interested in pop.

Mick Jagger

Now little Tom watched all these sweet things given away, till his mouth watered, and his eyes grew as round as an owl's. For he hoped that his turn would come at last; and so it did. For the lady called him up, and held out her fingers with something in them, and popped it into his mouth; and, lo and behold, it was a nasty cold hard pebble.

'You are a very cruel woman,' said he, and began to whimper.

'And you are a very cruel boy; who puts pebbles into the sea-anemones' mouths, to take them in, and make them fancy that they had caught a good dinner? As you did to them, so I must do to you.'

'Who told you that?' said Tom.

'You did yourself, this very minute.'

Tom had never opened his lips; so he was very much taken aback indeed.

'Yes; every one tells me exactly what they have done wrong; and that without knowing it themselves. So there is no use trying to hide anything from me. Now go, and be a good boy, and I will put no more pebbles in your mouth, if you put none in other creatures'.'

'I did not know there was any harm in it,' said Tom.

'Then you know now. People continually say that to me: but I tell them, if you don't know that fire burns, that is no reason that it should not burn you; and if you don't know that dirt breeds fever, that is no reason why the fevers should not kill you. The lobster did not know that there was any harm in getting into the lobster pot; but it caught him all the same.'

'Dear me,' thought Tom, 'she knows everything!' And so she did, indeed.

The Water Babies by Charles Kingsley

THANKS TO THE BBC

Mummie's shut the door at last, Mummie's
    really gone,
–Now she's in the drawing-room; she's turned
    the wireless on–
I'm glad the BBC has got an Opera on tonight–

'Cos John and me arranged at tea to have a
    pillow fight,
And pillow fights are bumping things that
    make a lot of noise.
  (I wonder if an Opera sounds as loud as Jack
    Payne's boys?)
Johnny won the pillow fight (I fell and banged
    my head).
So next we played a little game of 'bouncing
    on the bed'.
Then after we had cleared away the feathers
    off the floor
And sewn the pillow up again, we bounced a
    little more.
  . . . That Opera made a lot of noise –
  ooh! . . . lots more noise than us,
  I'm glad we've got a wireless now, it saves a
    lot of fuss!

Jennie Dunbar

Only Richard and Dillwyn didn't normally spend their money on lemon sherbets or lollipops like the other children. They bought cigarettes – five Woodbine in a pack for three ha'pence, and a box of matches, which they would get through during the course of the film, puffing away in the back of the stalls. Needless to say, both boys would have been skinned alive if their parents had ever discovered. So, if they happened to have any cigarettes left over when the time came to go, they grudgingly threw the remainder over the wooden bridge so that no one was ever the wiser.

One night, however, rather than throw the last precious Woodbine away, they decided to smoke it on the way home. But they had already jettisoned their matches. 'Never mind,' said Richie, then all of eight years old, 'there's a chap coming up there; go and ask him for a light.' So Dillwyn duly did as he was told. 'Got a light, mister?' he asked as the figure loomed up to him in the darkness.

'I've got a light, yes,' said a horribly familiar voice; and his father delivered the first good

hiding that Dillwyn ever remembers having for something that he (rather than Richard) had actually done.

Burton: The Man Behind the Myth by Penny Junor

J apanese children are told that if they tell a lie, an imp will pull out their tongue. The terror of the 'oni' running away with their tongue has kept many a child to the truth.

Sneeze on Monday, sneeze for danger;
Sneeze on Tuesday, kiss a stranger;
Sneeze on Wednesday, get a letter;
Sneeze on Thursday, something better;
Sneeze on Friday, sneeze for sorrow;
Sneeze on Saturday, see your sweetheart
    tomorrow.

I was always with my mom and we were very close. She used to turn things in the [bath] water for me – she used to put this little boat I had in the water and then she would make the water turn like a whirlpool by turning her finger around and around the boat . . . it used to make me dizzy!

I'd laugh and laugh and I wanted to do it myself. But what happened was that I would start turning the water around and the boat would flop over upside down and it'd sink. I never understood it – how she could keep it from sinking.

James Dean

The first time I opened the cupboard door I gasped in horror at what I saw lurking in a corner. It was an octopus with an elephant's trunk. I fully expected it to grab my ankle and drag me into the darkness. I fled. At night the fearsome monster joined the ghostly giant at the end of the bathroom corridor to haunt me in my dreams. I started using the garden

lavatory rather than pass the spare room to get to the one upstairs, and it wasn't long before my parents noticed. They got the truth out of me and laughed. Reluctantly I allowed Dad to lead me by the hand back into the room and up to the cupboard. The door opened and there was the monster as terrifying as ever. My father grabbed it. It seemed to writhe like a creature trapped in its lair on the ocean floor, throwing up a cloud of dust as camouflage. Its glassy eyes flashed with malice. The ribbed trunk swung towards me. I shuddered, tore myself away from my father's grasp and ran. He shouted something after me, a meaningless phrase drowned by my yell. The monster turned out to be a primitive gas mask, the sort they used to slip over the head and tie around the waist with ribbons.

A British Picture by Ken Russell

IT'S A LONG WAY UP IN THE DARK

I know there are Bears at the bend of the stairs
I'll whistle to show them that nobody cares.
    I'll walk past them slowly then p'raps it'll
    show
    Those Bears I'm not frightened (in case they
    don't know).
That bend *was* exciting, not one single Bear
(Because I was whistling) came out of its lair.

    I'm safe in my bedroom, I've shut the door
    tight,
    And finished undressing and turned out the
    light.

And as for those Bears at the bend of the stairs

They can't touch me now 'cos I've
    said
        all
            my
                prayers!

                                    Jennie Dunbar

INDEPENDENCE

I never did, I never did, I never *did* like
    'Now take care, dear!'
  I never did, I never did, I never *did* want
    'Hold-my-hand';
I never did, I never did, I never *did* think much
  of 'Not up there, dear!'
  It's no good saying it. They don't understand.

                      A. A. Milne

There was a place in childhood, that I
  remember well,
And there a voice of sweetest tone, bright fairy
  tales did tell,
And gentle words, and fond embrace, were
  given with joy to me,
When I was in that happy place upon my
  mother's knee.

                    Samuel Lover

Sometimes five-year-old Bud [Marlon] Brando would shinny up the mantelpiece, pose there, clutch his chest dramatically, and fall from some imagined Indian arrow. The family competed to see who could eat fastest, hold their breath longest, tell the biggest lies, or sink fastest in muddy sand before hollering for help. Bud delighted in exploring neighbourhood rubbish dumps looking for rusty bicycle wheels, abandoned corsets, broken umbrellas, hairbrushes, or dead birds and cats. When his pet chicken died, Dodie arranged for the bird to be buried near the river. Bud disinterred it and brought it back to the kitchen, depositing it on the table. He was sent back to bury it again (he didn't).

He often got into scraps with neighbourhood kids. He was as jumpy as a gopher on a hot griddle. Dodie said later, 'One day the mother of a little boy in our neighbourhood came to our house in a towering rage and complained Bud had been beating her son. As soon as Bud learned the boy was younger than he, and he was about six, he left him alone.

They became bosom friends, and [twenty years later] Bud was the best man at his wedding.'

Brando: the Unauthorised Biography
by Charles Higham

Surrealism had a great effect on me, because then I realised that my imagery and my mind wasn't insanity; that if it was insane, I belong in an exclusive club that sees the world in those terms. Surrealism to me is reality. Psychic vision to me is reality. Even as a child. When I looked at myself in the mirror or when I was twelve, thirteen, I used to literally trance out into alpha. I didn't know what it was called then. I found out years later there's a name for those conditions. But I would find myself seeing hallucinatory images of my face changing and becoming cosmic and complete. It caused me to always be a rebel.

John Lennon

The way to the railway was all downhill over smooth, short turf with here and there furze bushes and grey and yellow rocks sticking out like candied peel from the top of a cake.

The way ended in a steep run and a wooden fence – and there was the railway with the shining metals and the telegraph wires and posts and signals.

They all climbed on to the top of the fence, and then suddenly there was a rumbling sound that made them look along the line to the right, where the dark mouth of a tunnel opened itself in the face of a rocky cliff; next moment a train had rushed out of the tunnel with a shriek and a snort, and had slid noisily past them. They felt the rush of its passing, and the pebbles on the line jumped and rattled under it as it went by.

'Oh!' said Roberta, drawing a long breath; 'it was like a great dragon tearing by. Did you feel it fan us with its hot wings?'

'I suppose a dragon's lair might look very like that tunnel from the outside,' said Phyllis.

But Peter said:

'I never thought we should ever get so near to a train as this. It's the most ripping sport!'

'Better than toy engines, isn't it?' said Roberta.

The Railway Children by E. Nesbit

. . . Archibald, my safe old bear,
Whose woollen eyes looked sad or glad at me,
Whose ample forehead I could wet with tears,
Whose half-moon ears received my confidence,
Who made me laugh, who never let me down.
I used to wait for hours to see him move,
Convinced that he could breathe. One dreadful
    day
They hid him from me as a punishment:
Sometimes the desolation of that loss
Comes back to me and I must go upstairs
To see him in the sawdust, so to speak,
Safe and returned to his idolator.

from *Summoned by Bells* by John Betjeman

HIAWATHA'S CHILDHOOD

At the door on summer evenings
Sat the little Hiawatha;
Heard the whispering of the pine-trees,
Heard the lapping of the water,
Sounds of music, words of wonder;
'Minne-wawa!' said the pine-trees,
'Mudway-aushka!' said the water.

Saw the fire-fly, Wah-wah-taysee,
Flitting through the dusk of evening,
With the twinkle of its candle
Lighting up the brakes and bushes,
And he sang the song of children,
Sang the song Nokomis taught him:

'Wah-wah-taysee, little firefly,
Little, flitting, white-fire insect,
Little, dancing, white-fire creature,
Light me with your little candle,
Ere upon my bed I lay me,
Ere in sleep I close my eyelids!'

                    Henry Wadsworth Longfellow

'What's the use of a circus without an'mals?'

But William waved aside the objection.

'We can easy *get* an'mals,' he said. 'Why you c' hardly walk down the road without meeting an'mals. There's an'mals simply all over the world.'

'Yes, but they aren't *ours*,' said Henry, virtuously.

'Anyway,' said William, not pressing this point, 'we've *got* an'mals, haven't we? I've got Jumble an' Whitey, an' I c' easy collect some insects an' teach 'em tricks an' – an' there's Ginger's family's cat, an' –'

'An' my aunt's got a parrot,' put in Douglas.

'An' there's a pig in the field nex' our garden,' said Ginger eagerly. 'I bet I dress it up an' learn to ride it.'

Quite suddenly the circus seemed to be approaching the realms of possibility.

William in Trouble by Richmal Crompton

59

Grandpa Joe and Charlie were half running and half walking to keep up with Mr Wonka, but they were able to read what it said on quite a few of the doors as they hurried by. EATABLE MARSHMALLOW PILLOWS, it said on one.

'Marshmallow pillows are terrific!' shouted Mr Wonka as he dashed by. 'They'll be all the rage when I get them into the shops! No time to go in, though! No time to go in!'

LICKABLE WALLPAPER FOR NURSERIES, it said on the next door.

'Lovely stuff, lickable wallpaper!' cried Mr Wonka, rushing past. 'It has pictures of fruits on it – bananas, apples, oranges, grapes, pineapples, strawberries, and snozzberries . . .'

'*Snozzberries?*' said Mike Teavee.

'Don't interrupt!' said Mr Wonka. 'The wallpaper has pictures of all these fruits printed on it, and when you lick the picture of a banana, it tastes of banana. When you lick a strawberry, it tastes of strawberry. And when you lick a snozzberry, it tastes just exactly like a snozzberry . . .'

'But what *does* a snozzberry taste like?'

'You're mumbling again,' said Mr Wonka.
'Speak louder next time. On we go! Hurry up!'
Charlie and the Chocolate Factory
by Roald Dahl

From his earliest years, Alfred Hitchcock
was a loner and a watcher, an observer
rather than a participant. 'I don't remember
ever having a playmate,' he recalled as an
adult. At family gatherings: 'I would sit quietly
in a corner, saying nothing. I looked and
observed a great deal. I've always been that
way and still am. I was anything but
expansive. I was a loner – can't even remember
having had a playmate. I played by myself,
inventing my own games.'
*The Dark Side of Genius: The Life of
Alfred Hitchcock* by Donald Spoto

Pat-a-cake, pat-a-cake, baker's man!
Make me a cake as fast as you can;
Pat it, and prick it, and mark it with B,
Put it in the oven for Baby and me.

'It's not my tortoise. And I'm soaking wet.
My sandals are all slimy. You'll be sorry!'
she screeched.

Patiently I turned and looked up at her
against the morning.

'It's half yours,' I said politely, but coldly.
'Uncle Salmon gave it to us *both*. So it stands
to reason that it's *ours*. Not just mine.'

She shrugged, but was silent. I stared at her.
She suddenly bent and started to unbuckle her
sandal. 'Well, I don't want my half of it.
You've got the part with the head. That's the
best part.' She sat down in the wet shaking her
old brown sandal. I could see her knickers, but
I didn't bother to tell her. She was so rotten.

'Well, go on home and I'll look for him alone. And when I find him I'll have both halves and you'll have to lump it.' I turned and ran away down the hill . . . in case she tried to follow. She didn't, but she screeched again.

'The head part is the most interesting part. You said so. I don't like the tail part. And if I go home alone Aleford's stallion could get me.'

I reached the edge of the meadow and threw myself on to the grass under the ash tree and lay there looking at the sky and puffing a bit. It was quite a long run down from the top.

It was only yesterday evening that I had carefully washed his shell, and then put a little olive oil on it so that it shone and gleamed like a great golden brown pebble on the beach at Birling Gap. Only yesterday that he'd had the very innermost heart of a lettuce. The pale, yellowish-whitish bit. And only yesterday that Reg Fluke told me to put a little hole in her end of the shell and fix a bit of string to it. 'Then he won't wander,' he said.

But I didn't, and here we were in the dawn, searching for him, in vain it seemed.

A Postillion Struck by Lightning by Dirk Bogarde

'There you are!' cried the Toad, straddling and expanding himself. 'There's real life for you, embodied in that little cart. The open road, the dusty highway, the heath, the common, the hedgerows, the rolling downs! Camps, villages, towns, cities! Here today, up and off to somewhere else tomorrow! Travel, change, interest, excitement! The whole world before you, and a horizon that's always changing! And mind, this is the very finest cart of its sort that was ever built, without any exception. Come inside and look at the arrangements. Planned 'em all myself, I did!'

The Mole was tremendously interested and excited, and followed him eagerly up the steps and into the interior of the caravan. The Rat only snorted and thrust his hands deep into his pockets, remaining where he was.

The Wind in the Willows by Kenneth Grahame

The next time I visited Granny Stamp I clambered back on to the roof and found the plant flowering once more. I counted the bricks from the corner of the parapet, marked the two it was growing between and broke it off again. In October, when I longed for a big toy fort and soldiers ready early for Christmas in the shop windows next to Jolly's the grocer in St Leonard's Road, I climbed on to the roof for a third time and, to my astonishment, there was the Fire Weed growing stronger than ever, with white fluffy seeds waiting to be blown off by the wind. I was so excited by the magical powers of this little flower that I couldn't wait to tell Dad about it, but he wasn't really interested. My dad only began to open up to me when I was in my late twenties. But maybe this is commonplace? I know in the East they say: 'The Mother is the first Guru, the Father is the second Guru, and the Guru is the third Guru.'

Stamp Album by Terence Stamp

'I have been silly,' she said to him, at last. 'I ask your forgiveness. Try to be happy . . .'

He was surprised by this absence of reproaches. He stood there all bewildered, the glass globe held arrested in mid-air. He did not understand this quiet sweetness.

'Of course I love you,' the flower said to him. 'It is my fault that you have not known it all the while. That is of no importance. But you – you have been just as foolish as I. Try to be happy . . . Let the glass globe be. I don't want it any more.'

'But the wind –'

'My cold is not so bad as all that . . . The cool night air will do me good. I am a flower.'

'But the animals –'

'Well, I must endure the presence of two or three caterpillars if I wish to become acquainted with the butterflies. It seems that they are very beautiful. And if not the butterflies – and the caterpillars – who will call upon me? You will be far away . . . As for the large animals – I am not at all afraid of any of them. I have my claws.'

And, naively, she showed her four thorns.

Then she added:

'Don't linger like this. You have decided to go away. Now go!'

For she did not want him to see her crying. She was such a proud flower . . .

The Little Prince by Antoine de St-Exupéry

As I walked by myself,
And talked to myself,
  Myself said unto me:
Look to thyself,
Take care of thyself,
  For nobody cares for thee.

I answered myself,
And said to myself,
  In the self-same way to me:
Look to thyself,
Or not look to thyself,
  The self-same thing will be.

The time had come for my violin practice. I began twanging the strings with relish. Mother was still frying and rolling up pancakes; my brothers lowered their heads and sighed. I propped my music on the mantelpiece and sliced through a Russian Dance while sweet smells of resin mixed with lemon and fat as the dust flew in clouds from my bow. Now and then I got a note just right, and then Mother would throw me a glance. A glance of piercing, anxious encouragement as she side-stepped my swinging arm. Plump in her slippers, one hand to her cheek, her pan beating time in the other, her hair falling down about her ears, mouth working to help out the tune – old and tired though she was, her eyes were a girl's, and it was for looks such as these that I played.

'Splendid!' she cried. 'Top-hole! Clap-clap! Now give us another, me lad.'

So I slashed away at 'William Tell', and when I did that, plates jumped; and Mother skipped gaily around the hearthrug, and even Tony rocked a bit in his chair.

Cider With Rosie by Laurie Lee

Before he could even speak, he learned to make his wishes known by drawing. He would draw spirals which represented to him *churros*, 'the long, twisting, sugar-dusted fritters one buys hot from stalls all over Spain.' It must have seemed quite miraculous for a little boy to discover that he could get sugar-dusted fritters by drawing them.

At four he started magically giving birth to animals, flowers and strange creatures of his imagination by cutting them out of paper and projecting them against the wall like Chinese shadows. He even cut out a look-alike of the young man his aunt Heliodora was secretly in love with and projected it on the wall, making everybody in the house, all of whom, of course, knew her 'secret', burst into laughter – everybody, that is, except Heliodora, who blushed to her ears. At other times he would draw his creatures in pencil. The first word he had uttered was 'piz', his baby word for *lapiz*, a pencil. 'Piz, piz,' he demanded, and his mother would give him a pencil.

Picasso: Creator and Destroyer
by Arianna Stassinopoulos

She [Andy Warhol's mother] spent hours making flower sculptures out of tin cans, which she would sell for 25 to 50 cents. Andy recalled them fifty years later:

> The tin flowers she made out of those fruit tins, that's the reason why I did my first tin-can paintings. You take a tin can, the bigger the tin can the better, like the family ones that peach halves come in, and I think you cut them with scissors. It's very easy and you just make flowers out of them. My mother always had lots of cans around, including the soup cans. She was a wonderful woman and a real good and correct artist, like the primitives.

Warhol by Victor Bockris

INVOCATION OF PEACE

Deep peace, pure white of the moon to you;
Deep peace, pure green of the grass to you;
Deep peace, pure brown of the earth to you;
Deep peace, pure grey of the dew to you,
Deep peace, pure blue of the sky to you!
Deep peace of the running wave to you,
Deep peace of the flowing air to you,
Deep peace of the quiet earth to you.

'Fiona Macleod'

Racked with indecision, I searched the ranks before me as an old lady in a high-necked Edwardian frock waited impatiently for my threepenny piece. A regiment of Gurkhas marched side by side with a pack of polar bears. The Band of the Coldstream Guards played to a pride of lions on one side and a gaggle of geese on the other, all marching along in serried ranks, right foot forward. I'd picture my toys at home. A lead knight in armour with raised mace fighting an Indian with raised

tomahawk, a machine-gunner shooting at a pyramid, a Zulu with assegai contemplating a tank, a crocodile about to be run over by the Coronation coach, and cowboys having a shoot-out among the palm trees in my medieval wooden fort. In childhood we inhabit a world of wonderful contrasts that later we often come to see as bizarre and do our best to rearrange, with everything in its 'proper' place. Unusual juxtapositions we label surrealistic. Yet what is surrealism but a second childhood with Freudian overtones which we have to be re-educated to enjoy? – part of the tragedy of growing up.

A British Picture by Ken Russell

THE RAINBOW

My heart leaps up when I behold
A rainbow in the sky:
So was it when my life began;
So is it now I am a man;
So be it when I shall grow old,
    Or let me die!

The child is father of the man;
And I could wish my days to be
Bound each to each by natural piety.

William Wordsworth

All this made him feel hungry. As he still had in his pocket the coin for the collection, he went into a cakeshop to buy something to eat. To the balloon he said: 'Be good, Balloon. Wait here for me and don't go away.'

The balloon only went to the corner of the shop to warm itself in the sun. But that was already too far. For the boys of the day before had seen it and thought that now was the moment to catch it. Unseen, they drew near, leapt upon the balloon and ran off with it.

When Pascal came out of the cakeshop there was no balloon. He ran in every direction, searching the sky. The balloon had disobeyed him again! Without a doubt it had gone off for a walk. But though he called at the top of his voice, the balloon did not come back.

The gang had tied the balloon to a heavy string and were trying to train it. 'We could show this magic balloon at the fair,' said the leader. He threatened it with a stick: 'Come here or I'll burst you,' he cried.

Luckily, Pascal saw the balloon from the other side of the wall, desperately dragging at the end of a heavy string. He called to it.

As soon as it heard its master, it flew towards him. Pascal untied the string and ran off with the balloon at top speed.

The Red Balloon by Albert Lamorisse

How sweet to be a Cloud
    Floating in the Blue!
Every little cloud
Always sings aloud.

'How sweet to be a Cloud
    Floating in the Blue!'
It makes him very proud
To be a little cloud.

A. A. Milne

GOING TO SCHOOL

FIRST DAY AT SCHOOL

A millionbillionwillion miles from home
Waiting for the bell to go. (To go where?)
Why are they all so big, other children?
So noisy? So much at home they
must have been born in uniform
Lived all their lives in playgrounds
Spent the years inventing games
that don't let me in. Games
that are rough, that swallow you up.

And the railings.
All around, the railings.
Are they to keep out wolves and monsters?
Things that carry off and eat children?
Things you don't take sweets from?
Perhaps they're to stop us getting out
Running away from the lessins. Lessin.
What does a lessin look like?
Sounds small and slimy.
They keep them in glassrooms.
Whole rooms made out of glass. Imagine.

I wish I could remember my name
Mummy said it would come in useful.
Like wellies. When there's puddles.
Yellowwellies. I wish she was here.
I think my name is sewn on somewhere
Perhaps the teacher will read it for me.
Tea-cher. The one who makes the tea.

Roger McGough

I'm Popeye the sailor man, full stop,
I live in a caravan, full stop.
I open the door and fall through the floor,
I'm Popeye the sailor man, full stop,
Comma comma, dash dash, full stop.

from *The Singing Game* by Iona and Peter Opie

The morning came, without any warning, when my sisters surrounded me, wrapped me in scarves, tied up my bootlaces, thrust a cap on my head, and stuffed a baked potato in my pocket.

'What's this?' I said.

'You're starting school today.'

'I ain't. I'm stopping 'ome.'

'Now, come on, Loll. You're a big boy now.'

'I ain't.'

'You are.'

'Boo-hoo.'

They picked me up bodily, kicking and bawling, and carried me up to the road.

'Boys who don't go to school get put into boxes, and turn into rabbits, and get chopped up Sundays.'

I felt this was overdoing it rather, but I said no more after that. I arrived at the school just three feet tall and fatly wrapped in my scarves. The playground roared like a rodeo, and the potato burned through my thigh. Old boots, ragged stockings, torn trousers and skirts, went skating and skidding around me. The rabble closed in; I was encircled; grit flew in my face like shrapnel. Tall girls with frizzled hair, and huge boys with sharp elbows, began to prod me with hideous interest. They plucked at my scarves, spun me round like a top, screwed my nose, and stole my potato.

I was rescued at last by a gracious lady – the sixteen-year-old junior-teacher – who boxed a few ears and dried my face and led me off to The Infants. I spent that first day picking holes in paper, then went home in a smouldering temper.

'What's the matter, Loll? Didn't he like it at school, then?'

'They never gave me the present!'

'Present? What present?'

'They said they'd give me a present.'

'Well, now, I'm sure they didn't.'

'They did! They said: "You're Laurie Lee, ain't you? Well, just you sit there for the present." I sat there all day but I never got it. I ain't going back there again!'

Cider With Rosie by Laurie Lee

This is me e.g. nigel molesworth the curse of st custard's which is the skool i am at. It is uterly wet and weedy as i shall (i hope) make clear but of course that is the same with all skools.

e.g. they are nothing but kanes, lat. french. geog. hist. algy, geom, headmasters, skool dogs, skool sossages, my bro molesworth 2 and MASTERS everywhere.

The only good things about skool are the BOYS wizz who are noble brave fearless etc. although you hav various swots, bulies, cissies, milksops greedy guts and oiks with whom i am forced to mingle hem-hem.

In fact any skool is a bit of a shambles AS YOU WILL SEE.

Down With Skool by Geoffrey Willans

TO DAVID, ABOUT HIS EDUCATION

The world is full of mostly invisible things,
And there is no way but putting the mind's eye,
Or its nose, in a book, to find them out,

Things like the square root of Everest
Or how many times Byron goes into Texas,
Or whether the law of the excluded middle
Applies west of the Rockies. For these
And the like reasons, you have to go to school
And study books and listen to what you are
    told,
And sometimes try to remember. Though I
    don't know
What you will do with the mean annual rainfall
On Plato's Republic, or the calorie content
Of the Diet of Worms, such things are said to be
Good for you, and you will have to learn them
In order to become one of the grown-ups
Who sees invisible things neither steadily nor
    whole,
But keeps gravely the grand confusion of the
    world
Under his hat, which is where it belongs
And teaches small children to do this in their
    turn.

Howard Nemerov

81

JOHNNY'S POCKETS

Johnny collects
Conkers on strings,
Sycamore seeds
With aeroplane wings,
Green acorn cups,
Seaweed and shells,
Treasures from crackers
Like whistles and bells.

Johnny collects
Buttons and rings,
Bits of a watch,
Cog wheels and springs,
Half-eaten sweets,
Nuts, nails and screws.
That's why his pockets
Bulge out of his trews.

Alison Winn

Conkers is an old-fashioned game which hav been played by generations of british boys. You kno what hapens you pick up a huge horse chestnut which look absolutely super like a derby winner and put some string through it. Then you chalenge grabber or gilibrand who hav a conkerer of 20. You say weedy things like

Obbly obbly onker

My first conker

Hay ho hay nonny no ect.

Honour your oponent and turn round on the points of your toes. After that you whirl your conker round and hurl it at the dangling target hem-hem. Successful conkers are always shiveled and weedy. Wot hapens is that your conker either shaters into a milion pieces or flies through the nearest window crash crash tinkle tinkle. ('i shall make you pay from your poket-money, molesworth, not becos i *need* the money but becos you must face the conse-quences of your actions.')

How to be Topp by Geoffrey Willans

I'd been honest at Dovedale, if nothing else. But I began to realise that was foolish. So I started lying about everything.

People like me are aware of their so-called genius at ten, eight, nine. I always wondered, 'Why has nobody discovered me?' In school, didn't they see that I'm cleverer than anybody in this school? That the teachers are stupid, too? That all they had was information that I didn't need.

John Lennon

THE BAREFOOT BOY

Oh, for boyhood's painless play,
Sleep that wakes in laughing day,
Health that mocks the doctor's rules,
Knowledge never learned of schools.

John Greenleaf Whittier

THE SCHOOL CHILDREN

The children go forward with their little
   satchels.
And all morning the mothers have labored
to gather the late apples, red and gold,
like words of another language.

And on the other shore
are those who wait behind great desks
to receive these offerings.

How orderly they are – the nails
on which the children hang
their overcoats of blue or yellow wool.

And the teachers shall instruct them in silence
and the mothers shall scour the orchards for a
   way out,
drawing to themselves the gray limbs of the
   fruit trees
bearing so little ammunition.

Louise Glück

His mother would send him [Marlon] so well dressed. But by the time he reached the classroom, he would have had a scuffle of some sort in the playground. His shirttail would be out, his hair all tousled, like a curly chrysanthemum on top. Usually, he had been fighting for the underdog in the yard, the guy who seemed to be losing.

Brando by Charles Higham

WONDERS OF NATURE

My Grandmother said, 'Now isn't it queer,
That boys must whistle and girls must sing?
But that's how 'tis!' I heard her say –
'The same tomorrow as yesterday.'

Grandmother said, when I asked her why
Girls couldn't whistle the same as I,
'Son, you know it's a natural thing –
Boys just whistle, and girls just sing.'

Mowgli grew up with the cubs, though they, of course, were grown wolves almost before he was a child, and Father Wolf taught him his business, and the meaning of things in the Jungle, till every rustle in the grass, every breath of the warm night air, every note of the owls above his head, every scratch of a bat's claws as it roosted for a while in a tree, and every splash of every little fish jumping in a pool, meant just as much to him as the work of his office means to a business man. When he was not learning, he sat out in the sun and slept, and ate and went to sleep again; when he felt dirty or hot he swam in the forest pools; and when he wanted honey (Baloo told him that honey and nuts were just as pleasant to eat as raw meat) he climbed up for it, and that Bagheera showed him how to do. Bagheera would lie out on a branch and call, 'Come along, Little Brother,' and at first Mowgli would cling like the sloth, but afterward he would fling himself through the branches almost as boldly as the grey ape.

The Jungle Books by Rudyard Kipling

Tis a lesson you should heed,
   Try, try, try again;
If at first you don't succeed,
   Try, try, try again.

Once or twice though you should fail,
   Try again;
If at last you would prevail,
   Try again.
If we strive, 'tis no disgrace
Though we may not win the race;
What should you do in that case?
   Try again.

If you find your task is hard,
   Try again;
Time will bring you your reward,
   Try again.
All that other folks can do,
Why with patience should not you?
Only keep this rule in view–
   Try again.

To have success in mathematics, take a flat key and insert it in the book, letting it remain for twenty-four hours, wishing in the meantime to be able to do the problems.

When I was a little boy
    I had but little wit;
It is some time ago,
    And I've no more yet;
Nor ever, ever shall
    Until that I die,
For the longer I live
    The more fool am I.

Boys are capital fellows in their own way among their mates, but they are unwholesome companions for grown people.

Charles Lamb

A was an Archer, and shot at a frog;
B was a Butcher, and had a great dog;
C was a Captain, all covered with lace;
D was a Dunce, with a very sad face;
E was an Esquire, with pride on his brow;
F was a Farmer, and followed the plough;
G was a Gamester, and he had ill luck;
H was a Hunter, and hunted a buck;
I was an Innkeeper, who loved good grouse;
J was a Joiner, and built up a house;
K was a King, so mighty and grand;
L was a Lady, and had a white hand;
M was a Miser, and hoarded up gold;
N was a Nobleman, gallant and bold;
O was an Oyster-wench, and went about town;
P was a Parson, and wore a black gown;
Q was a Quaker, and would not bow down;
R was a Robber, and wanted a whip;
S was a Sailor, and lived in a ship;
T was a Tinker, and mended a can;
V was a Vintner, a very great man;
W was a Watchman, and guarded the door;
X was Expensive, and so became poor;
Y was a Youth, and did not love school;
Z was a Zany, a poor harmless fool.

Georgie Porgie, pudding and pie,
Kiss'd the girls and made them cry;
When the girls came out to play
Georgie Porgie ran away.

O Peggy Purey-Cust, how pure you were:
My first and purest love, Miss Purey-Cust!
Satchel on back I hurried up West Hill
To catch you on your morning walk to school,
Your nanny with you and your golden hair
Streaming like sunlight. Strict deportment
    made
You hold yourself erect and every step
Bounced up and down as though you walked
    on springs.
Your ice-blue eyes, your lashes long and light,
Your sweetly freckled face and turned-up nose
So haunted me that all my loves since then
Have had a look of Peggy Purey-Cust . . . .

          from *Summoned by Bells* by John Betjeman

Frank Lahiffe loved Mary O'Dwyer as well. It was an intolerable triangle. She probably loathed both of us, but, at the age of four, I was not in the least interested in her feelings. The nuns compounded my heartache by placing Mary in a desk between Lahiffe and me. Learning my letters, I would trace the 'D' with my finger. It was cut from sandpaper and stuck on light blue cardboard. We would close our eyes and feel the shape of the 'D' while mouthing its sound. 'Duh,' I muttered with the others, but my eyes were slits of guile, partly open to facilitate my observation of the nun. When she looked away, I darted to the next desk and planted a kiss on Mary's knee. She sat there, eyes clamped tight, now muttering, 'Fuh.'

Lahiffe, more absorbed by his rival than his alphabet, then repeated my manoeuvre, kissing la O'Dwyer's other knee. She burst into tears. 'Mary O'Dwyer, stop being a cissy,' said the nun, not bothering to enquire into the reasons for the four-year-old's distress. 'Guh,' said Lahiffe and I.

Is That It? by Bob Geldof

'Pooh, *promise* you won't forget about me, ever. Not even when I'm a hundred.'

Pooh thought for a little.

'How old shall *I* be then?'

'Ninety-nine.'

Pooh nodded.

'I promise,' he said.

Still with his eyes on the world Christopher Robin put out a hand and felt for Pooh's paw.

'Pooh,' said Christopher Robin earnestly, 'if I – if I'm not quite –' he stopped and tried again – 'Pooh, *whatever* happens, you *will* understand, won't you?'

'Understand what?'

'Oh, nothing.' He laughed and jumped to his feet. 'Come on!'

'Where?' said Pooh.

'Anywhere,' said Christopher Robin.

· · · · ·

So they went off together. But wherever they go, and whatever happens to them on the way, in that elevated place on the top of the Forest a little boy and his Bear will always be playing.

The House at Pooh Corner by A. A. Milne

SOURCES AND ACKNOWLEDGEMENTS
Extracts and poems reproduced by
permission are listed below.

Bacall, Lauren, *Lauren Bacall, By Myself* (Jonathan Cape)

Betjeman, John, *Summoned by Bells* (John Murray, Publishers, Ltd)

Bockris, Victor, *Warhol* (Hutchinson/Muller)

Bogarde, Dirk, *A Postillion Struck by Lightning* (Chatto & Windus)

Crompton, Richmal, *William in Trouble* (Pan Macmillan Children's Books)

Dahl, Roald, *Boy: Tales of Childhood* (by permission of Murray Pollinger, Jonathan Cape Ltd and Penguin Books Ltd)

Dahl, Roald, *Charlie and the Chocolate Factory* (by permission of Murray Pollinger and Penguin Books Ltd)

Geldof, Bob, *Is That It?* (Sidgwick & Jackson)

Gelis, Jacques, *History of Childbirth* (Blackwell)

Glück, Louise, 'The School Children' (Echo Press)

Guinness, Alec, *Blessings in Disguise* (Hamish Hamilton, 1985; copyright © Alec Guinness 1985; reproduced by permission of Hamish Hamilton Ltd)

Higham, Charles, *Brando* (Sidgwick & Jackson)

Junor, Penny, *Burton: The Man Behind the Myth* (Sidgwick & Jackson)

Lamorisse, Albert, *The Red Balloon*, translated by M. Barnes (reproduced by permission of HarperCollins Publishers Ltd)

Lee, Laurie, *Cider with Rosie* (Chatto & Windus)

Levenson, Claude B., *The Dalai Lama: A Biography* (Unwin Hyman)

McGough, Roger, 'First Day at School' (reprinted by permission of the Peters Fraser & Dunlop Group Ltd)

Milne, A. A., *The House at Pooh Corner* (reprinted by permission of Methuen Children's Books)

Milne, A. A., *Winnie-the-Pooh* (reprinted by permission of Methuen Children's Books)

Milne, A. A., 'Independence' and 'Lines and Squares' from *When We Were Very Young* (reprinted by permission of Methuen Children's Books)

Nemerov, Howard, 'To David, About His Education' (by permission of Mrs Margaret Nemerov)

Opie, Iona and Peter, *The Singing Game* (copyright © Iona Opie 1985; by permission of Oxford University Press)

Russell, Ken, *A British Picture* (copyright © Sitting

Duck Ltd 1989; reprinted by permission of William
Heinemann Ltd)

Sinatra, Nancy, *Frank Sinatra, My Father* (copyright ©
1985 by Nancy Sinatra; reproduced by permission
of Hodder & Stoughton Ltd)

Spoto, Donald, *The Dark Side of Genius: The Life of
Alfred Hitchcock* (Hutchinson/Muller)

Stamp, Terence, *Stamp Album* (first published in Great
Britain by Bloomsbury Publishing Ltd, 1987)

Stassinopoulos, Arianna, *Picasso: Creator and
Destroyer* (Weidenfeld & Nicolson)

St-Exupéry, Antoine de, *The Little Prince*, translated
by Katharine Woods (reprinted by permission of
William Heinemann Ltd)

Willans, Geoffrey, *Down with Skool* (by permission of
Tessa Sayle)

Winn, Alison, 'Johnny's Pockets' (Brockhampton
Press)